FATS, OILS, AND SWEETS

by Robin Nelson

Lerner Publications Company · Minneapolis

We need to eat many kinds
of food to be **healthy**.

We should not eat a lot of
fats, **oils**, and **sweets**.

Oil is a kind of fat.

Sweets have a lot of sugar.

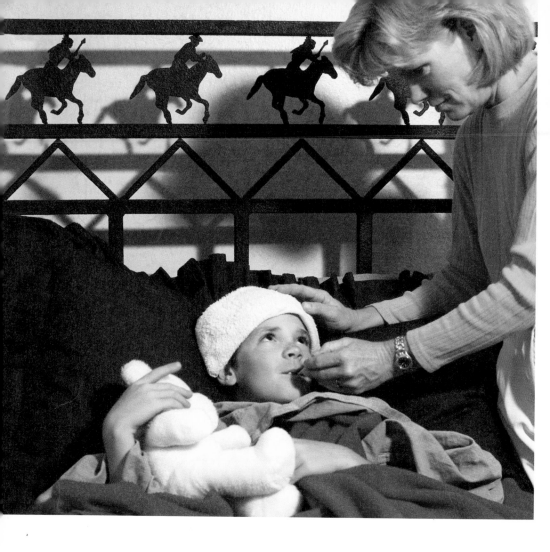

Too much fat and sugar
can make us sick.

Too much fat and sugar
can be **unhealthy**.

There are many snacks in
this group.

We should not eat too
many cookies.

We should not eat too
many french fries.

We should not drink too
much soda.

We can choose healthy
snacks.

We can eat popcorn.

We can eat vegetables.

We can eat fruits.

We can eat yogurt.

Watching what I eat keeps
me healthy.

Fats, Oils, and Sweets
Use Sparingly

Milk, Yogurt, and Cheese Group
2-3 Servings

Meat, Poultry, Fish, Dry Beans, Eggs, and Nuts Group
2-3 Servings

Vegetable Group
3-5 Servings

Fruit Group
2-4 Servings

Bread, Cereal, Rice, and Pasta Group
6-11 Servings

Fats, Oils, and Sweets

The food pyramid shows us how many servings of different foods we should eat every day. Fats, oils, and sweets are at the top of the food pyramid. This part of the pyramid is the smallest because you should not eat very many foods from this group. Many snacks like chips, cookies, candy, and soda belong to this group. The foods in this group taste good, but they have a lot of sugar or fat in them.

Fats, Oils, and Sweets Facts

 The most popular ice cream flavor is vanilla.

 The first chocolate chip cookie was invented by Ruth Graves Wakefield in 1930.

 Americans drink over 13 billion gallons of soft drinks each year.

 Each year, the most candy is sold during Halloween.

 Potato chips are Americans' favorite snack food.

Seven billion pounds of chocolate and candy are manufactured each year in the United States.

 Candy is the number one choice among children for an afternoon snack.

 If all the Easter jellybeans eaten by Americans in one year were lined end to end, they would circle the globe almost three times.

Glossary

 fats – parts of food that give you energy

 healthy – not sick; well

 oils – fatty liquids used in food

 sweets – foods that contain a lot of sugar and taste good

 unhealthy – sick; not well

Index

The photographs in this book are reproduced through the courtesy of: © Todd Strand/IPS, front cover, pp. 3, 4, 5, 8, 9, 11, 12, 13, 15, 17, 22 (top, middle, second from bottom); © PhotoDisc/ Royalty-Free, pp. 2, 7, 10, 22 (second from top); © Corbis Royalty-Free Images, pp. 6, 22 (bottom); © USDA/Bill Tarpenning, p. 14; © Midwest Dairy Association, p. 16.

Illustration on page 18 by Bill Hauser.

Lerner Publications Company
A division of Lerner Publishing Group
241 First Avenue North
Minneapolis, MN 55401 USA

Website address: www.lernerbooks.com

Library of Congress Cataloging-in-Publication Data

Nelson, Robin, 1971–
    Fats, oils, and sweets / by Robin Nelson.
        p.   cm. — (First step nonfiction)
    Summary: An introduction to fats and sweets and the part they play in a healthy diet.
    ISBN: 0–8225–4634–5 (lib. bdg. : alk. paper)
    1. Oils and fats—Juvenile literature. 2. Confectionery—Juvenile literature. 3. Nutrition— Juvenile literature. [1. Oils and fats, Edible. 2. Confectionery. 3. Nutrition.] I. Title. II. Series.
    TX560.F3 N45 2003
    641.3—dc21   2002013619

Manufactured in the United States of America
1 2 3 4 5 6 – JR – 08 07 06 05 04 03